PIRATE MOUSE
AND THE
LOST MAP

JON DUNCAN

Pirate Mouse and the Lost Map
Published by Last Rock Press
Denver, CO

Copyright ©2022 by Jon Duncan. All rights reserved.

No part of this book may be reproduced in any form or by any mechanical means, including information storage and retrieval systems without permission in writing from the publisher/author, except by a reviewer who may quote passages in a review.

All images, logos, quotes, and trademarks included in this book are subject to use according to trademark and copyright laws of the United States of America.

ISBN: 978-1-7378096-0-9
JUVENILE FICTION / Action & Adventure / Pirates

Publisher's Cataloging-in-Publication data

Names: Duncan, Jon, author.
Title: Pirate mouse and the lost map / Jon Duncan.
Description: Denver, CO: Last Rock Press, 2022. | Summary: A lost map to a hidden treasure has been found. Two friends are on a mission to get the map and find the treasure. Pirate Mouse and the Mummy escape capture and face a volcano.
Identifiers: ISBN 978-1-7378096-0-9
Subjects: LCSH Pirates--Juvenile fiction. | Maps--Juvenile fiction. | Treasure troves--Juvenile fiction. | Adventure stories. | BISAC JUVENILE FICTION / Action & Adventure / Pirates
Classification: LCC PZ7.1.D845 Pir 2022 | DDC [Fic]--dc23

Cover and Interior design by Victoria Wolf, wolfdesignandmarketing.com.
Copyright owned by Jon Duncan.
Illustrations by Jon Duncan.

QUANTITY PURCHASES: Schools, companies, professional groups, clubs, and other organizations may qualify for special terms when ordering quantities of this title. For information, email lastrockpress@gmail.com.

All rights reserved by Jon Duncan and Last Rock Press.
Printed in the United States of America.

TO THE SKITTLE DOLPHINS:
FOR THE LAUGHS, INSPIRATION, LOVE,
AND GENERAL SILLINESS
DURING A WILD TIME IN OUR LIVES.

ESCAPE FROM HARBORTOWN

THE OLD TOWN OF HARBORTOWN

A PEACEFUL OASIS AMONGST THE STORMY SEAS

WELL... MOST OF THE TIME...

THE VOLCANO

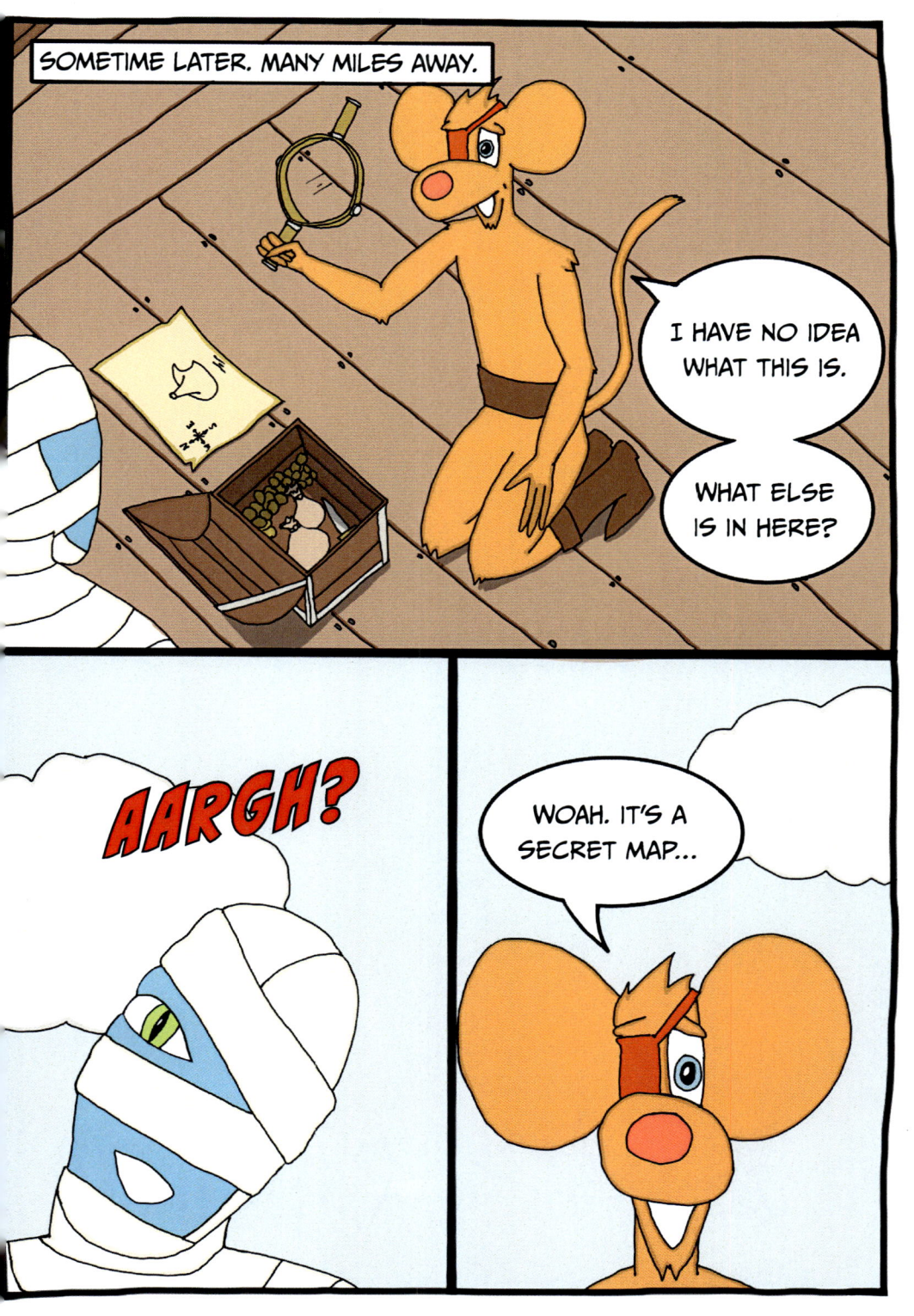

MORE
TALES OF PIRATE MOUSE

ABOUT THE AUTHOR

Jon Duncan is the author and illustrator of the award-winning Tales of Pirate Mouse, a graphic novel series based on adventure stories he created for his kids and their friends. Outside of drawing and writing, Jon enjoys snowboarding, hiking, camping, traveling, and daydreaming of new adventures. He lives in Denver with his wife, two kids, and dog.

Made in United States
Orlando, FL
22 December 2024

56443923R00033